# Decoding Deity

Unlocking the Mysteries of Numbers, Colors, Symbols, Names, & Places of the Bible

## By Pastor Bill Jenkins

Copyright © 2018

Church of ACTS Publishing
All rights reserved

Decoding Deity
Unlocking the Mysteries of Numbers, Colors, Symbols, Names, & Places of the Bible

By Pastor Bill Jenkins

ALL RIGHTS RESERVED
No part of this book may be reproduced, transmitted, or copied by any means, electronically or photo duplicated, without permission of the author. Unless otherwise noted, all scripture quotations are from the King James Version of the Bible.

Manufactured in the
United States of America
ISBN #978-0-578-40297-0

Published by
Church of ACTS Publishing
Indianapolis, Indiana

Visit the author's website:
www.pastorbilljenkins.org

# Table of Contents

Introduction ............................................................. 1

Chapter 1
Significant Numbers of the Bible ......................... 6
    Overview of Numbers ................................. 35

Chapter 2
Significant Colors of the Bible ............................ 37
    Overview of Colors ..................................... 59

Chapter 3
Significant Symbols of the Bible ........................ 60
    Objects ......................................................... 62
    Animals ....................................................... 65
    Signs ............................................................ 67

Chapter 4
Significant Names of the Bible .......................... 69
    Names of God ............................................. 69

Names of Jesus ................................................ 70
Names, or Symbols, of the Holy Spirit ........ 72
Names of Satan ............................................ 73
Names of Men .............................................. 74
Names of Women ......................................... 96

Chapter 5
Significant Places of the Bible ....................... 102
CONCLUSION .................................................. 114

# Introduction

Numbers, colors, symbols, names, and places are a language the Lord uses to communicate truth and revelation to His people. They have meaning that can give us further understanding of God's true intention for a particular passage of scripture in the Bible. *Decoding Deity* is not a complete effort to understand God Himself in His entirety. It is simply an attempt to convert some of the hidden and abstract messages of the Bible into understandable and applicable truth. I will use the Biblical references to unlock the mysteries of specific numbers, colors, symbols, names, and places. My goal is to help you not only determine the meaning behind these mysteries, but to increase your knowledge about God that is based on the scriptures. I also desire to make you more conscious when reading the Bible about looking for numbers, colors, symbols, names, and places. This will allow the Lord to expand your understanding of His great Word.

We are encouraged not just to read the Bible but study the Bible throughout scripture.

> *"Study to shew thyself approved unto God, a workman that needeth not to be ashamed, rightly dividing the word of truth." 2 Timothy 2:15*

> *"It is the glory of God to conceal a thing: but the honour of kings is to search out a matter." Proverbs 25:2*

Christians have an obligation to God to do more than just open up a Bible and read it. We should dig, search, invest, and put effort into obtaining greater knowledge from the Lord on a daily basis.

There are several innovative ways to study the Bible. It is good to use several approaches over a period of time both individually as well as in groups. Here are ten examples:

1. **Book or Passage-** Work directly from the Biblical text itself with no additional help.

Advantage: Direct exposure to the Word; avoiding a writer's possible bias.

2. **Deductive-** Use a Bible along with a guide book to help interpret.

   Advantage: Interpretation is already done; you just learn from a scholar.

3. **Inductive-** Use a Bible, and make a list of questions to ask and answer.

   Advantage: Excitement of digging out the meaning yourself.

4. **Relational-** Taking a Biblical text and putting yourself into the situation.

   Advantage: You experience the event.

5. **Character-** Study a specific personality.

   Advantage: You get to know Biblical characters better and their strengths and weaknesses.

6. **Doctrinal-** Study a particular doctrine.

Advantage: Learn the Biblical basis for doctrinal beliefs.

7. **Word-** Study a particular word.

   Advantage: See what words mean and how they are used.

8. **Topical-** Study a particular topic.

   Advantage: Gain insight into specific topics.

9. **Verse-** Study a particular verse.

   Advantage: get a deeper, more important message of a verse.

10. **Current issue-** Study of a current issue (abortion, poverty, race, hunger, etc.)

    Advantage: Relevance to life.

You can add the following approaches to that list: number study, color study, symbol study, name study, and place study.

## Eight Reasons Why We Study

1. To keep our relationship with the Lord fresh
2. To grow personally and become a better person
3. To gain deeper wisdom and greater insight from the Lord
4. To please the Lord
5. To know what to expect from God and what God expects of us
6. To give answers to others who ask questions
7. To be a part of God's inner circle
8. To walk in obedience to His Word

This book has tons of information and revelation that has taken hundreds of hours in study to acquire. However, there is more to be done. My desire is for everyone to search the Word more to discover the hidden secrets and unlock the mysteries God wants to reveal to us through His Word.

# Chapter 1
## Significant Numbers of the Bible

Studying Biblical numbers to search for their significance can only enhance our spiritual understanding and add to our continual growth in Christ. Numbers have meaning and the meaning of a number is determined by its connection and significance in a specific scripture to Biblical truths. In other words, the definition of a number is determined by the Biblical truth we conclude from a scripture.

Here are some numbers and their meanings according to God's numerical system:

**#1** = Singleness, unity, and beginnings.
- Absolute singleness of God, Deuteronomy 6:4
- The union of man and woman becoming one flesh, Genesis 2:24; Mark 10:7-9
- The desire of God for mankind, John 17:11
- The union of God, Ephesians 4:4-6

- The singleness of purpose in our lives, Luke 10:42
- Genesis is the number one book of the Bible and tells us of the beginning of mankind

**#2** = Witness, support, and agreement
- Two of every kind of animal entered the ark, Genesis 7
- Two Testaments make up the Word of God
- Two witnesses are required to validate a testimony, Deuteronomy 17:6; Matthew 26:60
- Two great lights to divide the day from the night, Genesis 1:5
- Two Commandments on which the Law and the Prophets hang upon, Matthew 22:40
- Two main masters in life (God and money), Matthew 6:24
- Two thieves on the Cross, Luke 23:39-43
- Two are better than one, Ecclesiastes 4:9

- Disciples sent two by two, Luke 10:1

**#3 = Completion and finish**

- Three close friends to Jesus, Luke 8:51-52; Mark 9:2-3
- Three times God spoke from heaven, Matthew 3:17, 17:5; John 12:28
- Three great enemies: the world, the flesh, and the devil, Ephesians 2:2-3
- Three temptations of man: lust of flesh, lust of eyes, and pride of life, 1 John 2:16
- Three great Christian characteristics: Faith, Hope, and Love, 1 Corinthians 13:13
- Three offices of Christ: Prophet, Priest, and King, Hebrews 6:20 & Hebrews 7
- Jonah was in a fish's belly for three days, Jonah 1:17
- Jesus' ministry lasted 3 years, Luke 13:7

**#4** = Earth-related number

- Four directions: North, South, East, and West
- Four seasons: Winter, Spring, Summer, and Fall
- Fourth book of Bible is Numbers, which deals with the wilderness journey of the believer
- On the fourth day of creation, the material world was finished, Genesis 1:14-19
- Four Gospels: Matthew, Mark, Luke, and John
- Four levels of Satanic influence: principalities, powers, rulers of darkness, and spiritual wickedness in high places

**#5** = Grace and favor

- Five wise virgins, Matthew 25:2
- Five loaves used to feed 5,000, Matthew 14:17
- Five-fold ministry: Apostle, Prophet, Evangelist, Pastor, and Teacher, Ephesians 4:11

- Five ingredients of Anointing Oil: myrrh, cinnamon, cane, cassia bark, and olive oil, Exodus 30:23-25
- Five sacrifices of Abraham: heifer, goat, ram, dove, and pigeon, Genesis 15:9
- Fifth time David is mentioned in 1 Samuel is in chapter 16 verse 22,

*"And Saul sent to Jesse, saying, Let David, I pray thee, stand before me; for he hath found favour in my sight."*

- David choose five smooth stones, 1 Samuel 17:40

**#6 = Man and Satan**

- Creation in Six days, Genesis 1:31
- Goliath was Six cubits (9 feet) tall, 1 Samuel 17:4
- Number of Anti-Christ is 666, Revelation 13:18
- Man was created on the sixth day, Genesis 1:24-31
- Man was to labor for six days before the Sabbath, Exodus 20:8-11
- Hebrew slaves were to serve for six years, Exodus 21:2

- Israel walked around the Wall of Jericho once a day for six days, Joshua 6:14-15

#7 = God's perfect number

- God rested on the seventh day, Genesis 2:2
- Jesus taught Peter to forgive 70x7, Matthew 18:22
- Seven sayings on the Cross, Luke 23:34,43, & 46; John 19:26-27; Matthew 27:46; John 19:28 & 30
- It took seven days to consecrate Aaron and his sons into the priesthood, Leviticus 8:31-35
- It was on the seventh day that Joshua and his army marched around the wall seven times, and it fell down, Joshua 6:15-20
- The mystery of God is finished when the seventh angel blows his trumpet, Revelations 10:7

#8 = New beginnings and new things

- Eight were saved from the flood, Genesis 7:13, 23

- Circumcision was to be performed on the eighth day, Genesis 17:12
- Thomas saw Jesus eight days after the resurrection, John 20:26
- God manifested His presence on the eighth day after seven days of consecration, Leviticus 23:36
- Dedication of babies were to take place eight days after birth in the House of the Lord, Exodus 22:29-30

#9 = Fruit and Fullness of Blessing

- Nine fruit of the Spirit, Galatians 5:22-23
- Nine people were stoned in the Bible
- Sara was 90 at the birth of Isaac, Genesis 17:17
- It was the ninth hour, the hour of prayer, when Peter and John made their way to the temple and brought healing to a lame man at the Gate of Beautiful, Acts 3:1
- Nine beatitudes, or attitudes, that "ought to be", Matthew 5:3-11

**#10 =** Law and Man's Government
- Ten Commandments, Exodus 20
- Malachi talks about giving a tithe or a tenth, Malachi 3:10
- A local government of ten men decided the fate of Ruth, Ruth 4:2

**#11 =** Disorder, offense, and confusion
- Eleven kings and rulers were offended with God's servants for declaring the truth:
    1. Pharaoh, Exodus 10:28
    2. Balak, Numbers 24:10
    3. Jeroboam, 1 Kings 13:4
    4. Ahab, 1 Kings 22:27
    5. Naaman, 2 Kings 5:11
    6. Asa, 2 Chronicles 16:10
    7. Joash, 2 Chronicles 24:21-22
    8. Uzziah, 2 Chronicles 26:19
    9. Jehoiakim, Jeremiah 26:21
    10. Zedekiah, Jeremiah 32:3
    11. Herod, Matthew 14:3
- Only Eleven disciples/apostles in Acts 1:26

- Eleven days journey from Mount Horeb to Kadesh-Barnea, Deuteronomy 1:2
- The Babylonians destroyed Jerusalem in the eleventh year of King Zedekiah, Jeremiah 39:2
- God gave Ezekiel a revelation about the destruction of Tyre in the eleventh year, Ezekiel 26:1
- Canaan had eleven sons, Genesis 10:15-18

**#12 = Divine Government**

- Twelve tribes, Genesis 49:1-28
- Twelve disciples, Luke 6:12-16
- Twelve gates and foundations in New Jerusalem, Revelation 21:12-14
- Twelve precious stones in Heaven, Revelation 21:19-21
- Twelve doctrines of Apostles, Acts 15
- Heaven is 12,000 furlongs, Revelation 21:16
- The wall in Heaven is 144 cubits high, which is 12x12, Revelation 21:17
- Solomon had twelve officers ruling in his household, 1 Kings 4:7

**#13** = Love, maturity, power, and rebellion

- Three books of the Bible have 13 chapters: Nehemiah, 2 Corinthians, Hebrews
- Ishmael was 13 when he was circumcised, Genesis 17:25
- Matthias was the 13th Apostle, Acts 1:26
- The first occurrence of 13 in the Bible is Genesis 14:4, *"Twelve years they served Chedorlaomer, and in the thirteenth year they rebelled."*

**#14** = Number of David and deliverance

- In Hebrew, there are no vowels, so in English, it's spelled, DAVID, but in Hebrew, it is spelled DVD. Every letter has a number attached to it, so the D = 4, and the V = 6. It totals up to 14.
- The 14th time Jesus is mentioned in the gospel of Luke is in Luke 4:35 where Jesus delivered a man from a demon
- The 14th time Abram is mentioned in scripture is Genesis 12:10 where

Abram went down to Egypt to deliver himself from the famine in Canaan.

**#15** = Rest, God-Sends, addition, and extension

- Fifteen in Hebrew is two Hebrew letters, Yod-Hey, which signifies the Hand of God or the outworking/outpouring of the Holy Spirit
- Genesis 15:15 is symbolic of extending and enjoying life
- Psalm 15 speaks of God's rest
- In 2 Samuel 9:10, Ziba who was Saul's servant, kept adding to his family; he had 15 sons
- Hezekiah was given a 15 year extension to his life, 2 Kings 20:4-6

**#16** = Love

- 16 characteristics of love in 1st Corinthians 13:4-8
- The 16th time Love is used is in 1st John; it declares there is no fear in Love, 1st John 4:18

- In the Old Testament there are 16 names of God that specifically refer to His unending love for Israel
- Sixteen is made of two Hebrew letters, Yod-Vay: The hand of God that joins two people as one
- The 16th time Noah is mentioned it speaks of marriage, *"They went into the Ark by two, male and female."* Genesis 7:9a paraphrased
- The 16th time Abram is mentioned is Genesis 12:16 where Pharaoh loved Sarah and took her into his harem
- The book of John uses the Greek word agape, "divine love", 16 times

#17 = Resetting your life and victory

- Jesus gained complete victory over death, hell, and the grave when He was resurrected on Nisan 17
- Psalm 83:6-11 mentions 17 total enemies that have been or would be defeated
- The flood started on the 17th day in Genesis 7:11
- Noah's Ark came to rest on Mount Ararat on the 17th day, Genesis 8:4

- The Old Testament has 17 Historical Books
- The Old Testament has 17 Prophetic Books

#18 = Bondage and Oppression

- Israel's enemies, Eglon, the Moabite King and the Philistines, oppressed them for 18 year, Judges 3:10-14
- Jesus healed a woman of a spirit of infirmity that she had for 18 years, Luke 13:10-17
- The Ammorites oppressed Israel for 18 years, Judges 10:8
- 18 People killed by the fall of the Tower at Siloam, Luke 13:4

#19 = Conflict and faith

- In 2 Samuel 2:30, there was a war in which Abner the enemy lost 360 men and David lost 19 men.
- 19 people listed in the Hall of Fame of Faith, Hebrews 11

- From Romans 3:21 to Romans 5:2, Paul uses the word "faith" 19 times in discussion of us being justified by faith
- The 19th time Abram is mentioned is in Genesis 13:1 where he leaves Egypt and returns to Canaan.

#20 = Judgment

- Samson was judge over Israel for 20 years, Judges 15:20
- The Israelite men who were numbered in the census had to be 20 years of age, Exodus 30:14
- There are 20 boards on each side (North and South) of Moses' Tabernacle, Exodus 26:18-19
- The outer court of the Tabernacle was surrounded by a wall anchored by 20 pillars, Exodus 26:20
- The 20th time Abraham is mentioned is in Genesis 18:23, *"And Abraham drew near, and said, Wilt thou also destroy the righteous with the wicked?"*
- 20 different people are mentioned in the Book of Ruth which is the story of the Kinsman-Redeemer

**#21 = Great Wickedness**

- Israel committed 21 sins that were recorded against them during their 40 years in the wilderness. The tabernacle had 21 coverings to cover all their sins, Exodus 26:3-7
- The 21$^{st}$ time Joshua is mentioned is in Deuteronomy 31:3 where Moses told the people of Israel that Joshua would be leading them into the promised land
- Jacob had two great times of distress that lasted 21 years, Genesis 29; Genesis 35

**#22 = Disorder and confusion**

- There are 22 almonds on seven branches of the candlestick in the tabernacle, Exodus 25: 31-37
- There are 22,000 priests of Levi that redeemed the firstborn sons of Israel, Numbers 3:39
- Solomon offered 22,000 sheep to God when he dedicated the temple, 2 Chronicles 7:5
- In the New Testament book of Acts, Saul is mentioned 22 times

- The 22<sup>nd</sup> time David is mentioned in the Bible he is delivering the lambs from the lions and the bears, 1 Samuel 17:34
- There are 22 letters in the Hebrew alphabet
- Jesus quotes the opening of Psalm 22 while in agony on the cross, "My God, my God, why hast thou forsaken me?"
- Jeroboam reigned for 22 years
- Revelation ends the whole Bible on a 22nd chapter

#23 = Greatness

- There are 23 things "worthy of death" in Romans 1:28-32
- The 23<sup>rd</sup> time Israel is mentioned is in Genesis 47:31 where he had just given instructions to Joseph on where to bury him when he dies.
- The 23<sup>rd</sup> time Jerusalem is mentioned is in 2 Samuel 10:14 where it mentions how David returned from battle. Over 40,000 were killed.

**#24 = Priesthood and leadership**
- The gospel of Luke has 24 chapters, and it gives us a lot of priestly duties to live by
    - There are 24 elders around the throne of God assisting in the governing of the world, Revelation 4:1-4
    - Baasha, who was the 3rd King of Israel, reigned 24 years, 1 Kings 15:33
    - Psalm 72 lists 24 things that Jesus, who is a High Priest after the order of Melchizedek, will do as King and Priest during the Millennium reign
        1. Judge righteously
        2. Judge the needy
        3. Bring peace to the mountains
        4. Bring peace to the lower plains
        5. Judge the poor
        6. Save the children of the needy
        7. Crush the oppressors
        8. Water the grass
        9. Rule all over the globe
        10. Cause the righteous to flourish
        11. Give peace to the righteous ones
        12. Rule from sea to sea
        13. Rule from river to the end of the earth
        14. Deliverance to the poor
        15. Release compassion

16. Save those in need
17. Redeem us from violence
18. Reward the righteous
19. Abundance of grain
20. Abundance of fruit
21. Cities will flourish
22. His name will live forever
23. Bless all mankind
24. Hear the cry and bring deliverance to the needy

**#25** = Forgiveness and multiplied grace

- Five is the number of grace, and to get to 25 you multiply 5x5, so it's grace multiplied
- Levites were to begin to serve at the age of 25 in assisting with sacrifices that represent forgiveness, Numbers 8:24
- King Jehoshaphat ruled for 25 years, 1 Kings 22:42
- King Amaziah began his reign at age 25, 2 Kings 14:2

**#26 = House of God**

- The width and length of the House of God was to be 26 cubits, 1 Kings 6:2
- Psalm 26 commemorates David's return to the House of God

**#27 = Fullness of Spirit**

- 27 books in the New Testament
- The 27$^{th}$ word of the Bible is, "deep". There was a hole in the world and a hole in our heart that should only be filled with the Spirit of God.

**#28 = Leading of the Holy Spirit**

- The book of Acts has 28 chapters and is the longest book in the New Testament. It is about learning to be led by the Holy Spirit.
- We are given 28 "times" or "seasons" we will be led into during our life:

| | |
|---|---|
| - A time to be born | - A time to die |
| - A time to plant | - A time to pluck |
| - A time to kill | - A time to heal |
| - A time to break | - A time to build |
| - A time to weep | - A time to laugh |

- A time to mourn — A time to dance
- A time to cast stones — A time to gather stones
- A time to embrace — A time to refrain
- A time to get — A time to lose
- A time to keep — A time to cast away
- A time to rend — A time to sew
- A time to keep silent — A time to speak
- A time to love — A time to hate
- A time for war — A time for peace

- 28th time Noah is mentioned in the Bible is Genesis 8:15, where God leads him to "go out of the Ark"

#29 = Departure

- The 29th time Abram is mentioned in the Bible is Genesis 14:12 where he then goes on to depart from the Kings of Sodom and Gomorrah
- The 29th time Jacob is mentioned in the Bible is Genesis 28:7 where he left his parents
- The 29th time Jesus is mentioned in the Bible is Matthew 8:34 where the people wanted Him to depart after healing the demoniac

**#30** = Sorrow and mourning

- Israel mourned Moses' death for 30 days, Deuteronomy 34:8
- Israel mourned Aarons death for 30 days, Numbers 20:29
- Judas betrayed Jesus for 30 pieces of silver, Matthew 26:15
- The usual price for a slave was 30 pieces of silver, Exodus 21:32

**#31** = Fruitfulness and reproduction

- The 31st time Noah is mentioned in the Bible is in Genesis 8:1-17 where God tells him, "to be fruitful and multiply."
- The 31st time Isaac is mentioned in the Bible is in Genesis 25:26 which refers to giving birth

**#32** = Covenant

- Psalm 32 is about God's covenant with mankind
- 32 degrees Fahrenheit is the freezing point of water. It's a "law of life" or a "covenant that will last forever".

**#33** = Divine fulfillment

- Jesus was crucified at 33 years old
- David reigned as king of Jerusalem for 33 years, 1 Kings 2:11

**#34** = Breaking barrenness

- Deuteronomy has 34 chapters and is about how obedience to God breaks barrenness
- Jacob's first wife, Leah, is mentioned 34 times in scripture and had her barrenness removed

**#35** = Prayer and praise

- Jehoshaphat was 35 years old when he began to reign in 1 Kings 22:42, and he lead the nation back to God in prayer and praise
- Two pillars outside of the tabernacle were 35 cubits high, 2 Chronicles 3:15

**#36 = Sin revealed**

- Psalm 36 is about getting your heart right with God before your secret sin gets revealed
- 36 people were killed in Joshua 7 because of secrets and disobedience to God

**#37 = Strength**

- David had 37 mighty men of strength and valor, 2 Samuel 23:39

**#38 = Ending**

- Azariah, king of Judah, reigned 38 years, 2 Kings 15:8
- Asa, king of Judah, reigned 38 years, 1 Kings 16:29
- An entire generation of Israelites died in the wilderness over a 38 year period of time, Deuteronomy 2:14

**#40 = Testing and trial**

- It rained 40 days during the flood, Genesis 7:4

- Jesus spent 40 days in the wilderness, Matthew 4:2
- Israel had to wander in the wilderness for 40 years because of their unfaithfulness, Numbers 14:33
- Jesus and Moses fasted for 40 days and nights, Matthew 4:2; Exodus 34:28
- The rain fell for 40 days and 40 nights during the flood of Noah's day, Genesis 7:12
- The Israelite spies were in the land of Canaan for 40 days and nights
- Jesus was seen after His resurrection for 40 days, Acts 1:3
- The prophet Ezekiel laid on his right side for 40 days to symbolize Judah's sins, Ezekiel 4:6
- After Moses killed the Egyptian, he fled to Midian where he spent 40 years in the wilderness, Exodus 3; Acts 7:30
- It was a 40 day wait for embalming a body in the Old Testament, Genesis 50:3
- 40 stripes were often administered to a criminal as punishment, Deuteronomy 25:3

- Saul, David, and Solomon all ruled as king for 40 years

#50 = Celebration

- The 50th year was a jubilee to Israel. On the Day of Atonement, a jubilee was declared with the sound of a trumpet, Leviticus 25:9 & 10
- Pentecost occurred 50 days after Christ's resurrection, Acts 2
- The fourth longest book in the entirety of Scripture is Genesis with its 50 chapters
- Noah's Ark was 300 cubits long, 30 cubits high, and 50 cubits deep, Genesis 6:15
- The work of maintaining God's tabernacle in the wilderness was so laborious that only men who were between 30 and 50 years old were allowed to serve, Numbers 4:1-3
- There was a penalty in ancient Israel that if an unmarried man had sex with a virgin who was not engaged to be married, his penalty was to pay the woman's father 50 shekels of silver, and he had to marry her. He was not

- allowed to 'put her away' or divorce her as long as she lived, Deuteronomy 22:28-29
- King David paid 50 shekels of silver to purchase the threshing floor where a death angel was told to stop and not destroy Jerusalem, 2 Samuel 24:24
- The gallows which Haman built for the use of having his enemy Mordecai executed upon was 50 cubits high, Esther 5:14, 7:9
- God promised Abraham that if he found only 50 righteous people in Sodom and Gomorrah, He would not destroy both cities, Genesis 18:23 – 26

#65 = Division

- Mahalaleel, the great, great grandson of Adam, and Enoch, the seventh generation of man, were both 65 years old when they had their first son.
- The number 65 is associated to the downfall of the tribe of Ephraim. Isaiah the prophet stated, *"...Within threescore and five years shall Ephraim be broken...",* Isaiah 7:8

- +65 is the international calling code for Singapore
- Singapore separated from Malaysia and became independent on August 9, 1965

**#70 = Divine committees**

- Moses appointed 70 elders, Numbers 11:16
- After reading the covenant God gave him to read to the people, Moses took 70 elders, along with Aaron and his sons, up to Mount Sinai to have a special meal with God himself, Exodus 24:9-11
- Ancient Israel spent a total number of 70 years in captivity in Babylon, Jeremiah 29:10
- 70 is also specially connected with Jerusalem. The city kept 70 years of Sabbaths while Judah was in Babylonian captivity, Jeremiah 25:11
- 70 weeks were determined upon Jerusalem for it to complete its transgressions, to make an end for sins, and for everlasting righteousness to enter into it, Daniel 9:24

- Terah, the father of Abraham (who was not his oldest son), had his first male child at 70, Genesis 11:26
- Cainan had his first son at the age of 70, Genesis 5:12
- Israel in Egypt had its beginnings with Joseph rising in power in Pharaoh's court and Jacob migrating his entire household into the land. A total of 70 Israelites started a nation within another nation that would grow to more than two million by the Exodus
- Seventy disciples were sent out by Christ on a mission to preach the gospel and release the power of God, Luke 10:1
- The prophet Ezekiel was taken by God, in a vision, to Jerusalem to be shown 70 elders of Israel defiling themselves by offering incense to their idols, Ezekiel 8

**#120** = Waiting

- After God saw how sinful and dedicated to evil man had become after the garden of Eden, He determined a one hundred and twenty

year period would be given for repentance and then the flood waters would come, Genesis 6:1-3
- After Jesus' resurrection and ascension to heaven, 120 disciples that were gathered in Jerusalem chose a successor to Judas Iscariot (who committed suicide) to be among the special eleven disciples who were witnesses of Christ's entire ministry, Acts 1:14 – 26

## Overview of Numbers

| | | |
|---|---|---|
| 1 | = | Singleness, unity, and beginnings |
| 2 | = | Witness, support, and agreement |
| 3 | = | Completion and finish |
| 4 | = | Earth-Related number |
| 5 | = | Grace and favor |
| 6 | = | Man and Satan |
| 7 | = | God's perfect number |
| 8 | = | New beginnings and new things |
| 9 | = | Fruit and fullness of blessing |
| 10 | = | Law and man's government |
| 11 | = | Disorder, offense, and confusion |
| 12 | = | Divine government |
| 13 | = | Love, maturity, power, and rebellion |
| 14 | = | Number of David and deliverance |
| 15 | = | Rest, God-Sends, addiction, and extension |
| 16 | = | Love |
| 17 | = | Resetting your life and victory |
| 18 | = | Bondage and oppression |
| 19 | = | Conflict and faith |
| 20 | = | Judgment |
| 21 | = | Great wickedness |
| 22 | = | Disorder and confusion |
| 23 | = | Greatness |

| | | |
|---|---|---|
| 24 | = | Priesthood and leadership |
| 25 | = | Forgiveness and multiple grace |
| 26 | = | House of God |
| 27 | = | Fullness of Spirit |
| 28 | = | Leading of the Holy Spirit |
| 29 | = | Departure |
| 30 | = | Sorrow and mourning |
| 31 | = | Fruitfulness and reproduction |
| 32 | = | Covenant |
| 33 | = | Divine fulfillment |
| 34 | = | Breaking barrenness |
| 35 | = | Prayer and praise |
| 36 | = | Sin revealed |
| 37 | = | Strength |
| 38 | = | Ending |
| 40 | = | Testing and trial |
| 50 | = | Celebrations |
| 65 | = | Division |
| 70 | = | Divine committees |
| 120 | = | Waiting |

# Chapter 2
## Significant Colors of the Bible

### Blue

The color blue represents Heaven. Blue is the color of the sky, and it is a reminder of what is to come when we get to Heaven.

The word Heaven, or Heavens, is used 718 times and refers to the place God dwells.

Heaven is a place of:
1. Holiness, Revelation 21:27
2. Exceptional Beauty, Psalm 50:2
3. Unity, Ephesians 1:10
4. Perfection, 1 Corinthians 13:10
5. Joy & Pleasure, Psalm 16:11

In Heaven there will not be everything; there will be some things absent or missing. There will be no tears, sickness, pain, death, no more famine, no more thirst or hunger, no sin, no judgment for sin, no night, no sun or moon, and no light will be needed because Jesus is the light, Revelation 21:23

- The Father will be there, Revelation 4:2-3
- The Son will be there, Revelation 5:6; 7:17
- The Holy Spirit will be there, Revelation 14:13; 22:17
- We will share Heaven with Redeemed Israel, Hebrews 11:10, 16
- We will share Heaven with Angels, Hebrews 12:22, Revelation 5:11
- The River of Life is there to ensure everlasting life, Revelation 22:1
- The Tree of Life is there to ensure abundant life, Revelation 2:7; 22:19
- The Tree of Life will bear different fruit each month (figs, sycamore fruit, grapes, melons), Revelation 22:2
- The Throne of God will occupy the central palace, Revelation 4:2; 22:1. It is likened to burning wheels of fire with an emerald (rich green, prosperity, and growth)
- The Golden Altar is there with bowls of incense, Revelation 5:8
- The Menorah or 7-branched lampstand is there, Revelation 1:12
- Around the throne are four special angels with the faces of: 1. Lion, 2.

Calf, 3. Man, 4. Eagle; these represent four kinds of worship, Revelation 4:7
- Revelation 1:20 Mentions
  Seven Candlesticks = Seven Churches
  Seven Stars = Angels assigned to assist in warfare

**Six Different Names of Heaven**

1. The Holy City, Revelation 21:2
2. New Jerusalem, Revelation 21:2
3. The Tabernacle of God, Revelation 21:3
4. The Holy Jerusalem, Revelation 21:10
5. The Heavenly Jerusalem, Hebrews 12:22
6. The Father's House, John 14:2-3

*"And they saw the God of Israel: and there was under his feet as it were a paved work of a sapphire stone, and as it were the body of heaven in his clearness." Exodus 24:10*

*"And above the firmament that was over their heads was the likeness of a throne, as the appearance of a sapphire stone: and upon the likeness of the throne was the likeness as the*

*appearance of a man above upon it."*
*Ezekiel 1:26*

In both of those scriptures the sapphire stone is mentioned in connection with heaven. Sapphires are blue in color and reflect the beauty of Heaven.

## **Black**

The color black is often used to represent mourning and death:

> *"I went mourning without the sun: I stood up, and I cried in the congregation. I am a brother to dragons, and a companion to owls. My skin is black upon me, and my bones are burned with heat." Job 30:28-30*

> *"Judah mourneth, and the gates thereof languish; they are black unto the ground; and the cry of Jerusalem is gone up." Jeremiah 14:2*

> *"Before I go whence I shall not return, even to the land of darkness and the shadow of death; A land of darkness, as darkness itself; and of the shadow*

*of death, without any order, and where the light is as darkness." Job 10:21-22*

The color black absorbs lights and never reflects light. Light was the first thing created by God to divide the darkness and bring color to the world. The Bible tells us God is light.

*"This then is the message which we have heard of him, and declare unto you, that God is light, and in him is no darkness at all." 1 John 1:5*

Prior to Satan's fall from Heaven because of rebellion, he was known as, the "angel of light", but he fell from Heaven like lightning and now exists in darkness. (Luke 10:18)

*"For the wages of sin is death; but the gift of God is eternal life through Jesus Christ our Lord." Romans 6:23*

**Black is used in Bible in connection with:**

- Hair, Song of Solomon 5:11
- Horses, Revelation 6:5

- Heavens, 1 Kings 18:45
- Sun, Revelation 6:12
- Skin, Song of Solomon 1:5-6
- Pavement, Esther 1:6
- Passion, Jeremiah 8:12

## Yellow

Yellow is one of the seven colors found in a rainbow. Traffic lights and signs are yellow to symbolize caution when traveling. Yellow is also the color of the sun and represents joy and warmth. Yellow is a primary color but is also connected sometimes with the color gold.

> *"Though ye have lien among the pots, yet shall ye be as the wings of a dove covered with silver, and her feathers with yellow gold." Psalm 68:13*

Yellow is also used to describe someone with leprosy or something that had a disease attached to it.

Leviticus 13:30, 32, and 36

> Verse 30, *"Then the priest shall see the plague: and, behold, if it be in sight deeper than the skin; and there be in it a*

*yellow thin hair; then the priest shall pronounce him unclean: it is a dry scall, even a leprosy upon the head or beard."*

Verse 32, *"And in the seventh day the priest shall look on the plague: and, behold, if the scall spread not, and there be in it no yellow hair, and the scall be not in sight deeper than the skin;"*

Verse 36, *"Then the priest shall look on him: and, behold, if the scall be spread in the skin, the priest shall not seek for yellow hair; he is unclean."*

Yellow is connected to Frankincense, which is yellow in color and was one of the gifts the wise men brought to Jesus. The New Jerusalem has 12 foundations, and the seventh foundation is made with chrysolite gemstone, and it is yellow in color. Anointing Oil is yellow in color and it removes burdens from our lives through the power in Jesus Christ.

## Gold

Gold is a precious metal and can be extremely valuable. Gold points to the supremacy of God and great prosperity when it is mentioned in the Bible. In the Old Testament, kings and great leaders wore gold to signify their position of authority. They would surround themselves with items of gold to proclaim their power and wealth.

- King Solomon had an ivory throne overlaid with gold, 1 Kings 10:18
- The Ark of the Covenant was made of Acacia wood but was overlaid with pure gold, Exodus 25:11
- The mercy seat was also made of gold, Exodus 25:10-21
- The streets of Heaven are paved in gold, Revelation 21:21

## Red

The color red in the Bible represents blood, redemption, sacrifice, and love. The life of mankind is in the blood.

> *"For the life of the flesh is in the blood: and I have given it to you upon the altar to make an atonement for your souls: for it is the blood that maketh an atonement for the soul."* Leviticus 17:11

It is only through the precious Blood of Jesus that was sacrificed on the cross that redeems us and makes us one with Christ. Jesus' shed blood paid the penalty for our sins, and by the blood of Jesus we are washed clean.

> *"And, having made peace through the blood of his cross, by him to reconcile all things unto himself; by him, I say, whether they be things in earth, or things in heaven. And you, that were sometime alienated and enemies in your mind by wicked works, yet now hath he reconciled"* Colossians 1:20-21

> *"In whom we have redemption through his blood, the forgiveness of sins, according to the riches of his grace;"* Ephesians 1:7

Through the shed blood of Christ offered for us to receive eternal life, the Lord gave us the greatest show of sacrifice and love.

> *"Greater love hath no man than this, that a man lay down his life for his friends." John 15:13*

- Adam was made from dust, or clay, which was red, Genesis 2:7
- Red linen was used in the Tabernacles, Exodus 25:4

## **Purple**

Purple represents royalty and wealth. In the Old Testament, purple dye was very expensive and could only be purchased by the rich and powerful people of the land.

> *"And the weight of the golden earrings that he requested was a thousand and seven hundred shekels of gold; beside ornaments, and collars, and purple raiment that was on the kings of Midian, and beside the chains that were about their camels' necks." Judges 8:26*

*"And a certain woman named Lydia, a seller of purple, of the city of Thyatira, which worshipped God, heard us: whose heart the Lord opened, that she attended unto the things which were spoken of Paul." Acts 16:14*

*"She maketh herself coverings of tapestry; her clothing is silk and purple." Proverbs 31:22*

*"Fine linen with broidered work from Egypt was that which thou spreadest forth to be thy sail; blue and purple from the isles of Elishah was that which covered thee." Ezekiel 27:7*

The color purple is made by mixing the colors of red and blue. Remember, red represents redemption and blue represents Heaven, so purple, or true wealth and power, comes when Jesus redeems us and gives us the promise of Heaven.

## **Gray**

When gray is mentioned in the Bible, it refers to one of two things: the first is the weakness that occurs when we get older in age. The second is the wisdom we have obtained that we can offer to others to help them avoid trouble or find blessing.

> "And he said, My son shall not go down with you; for his brother is dead, and he is left alone: if mischief befall him by the way in the which ye go, then shall ye bring down my gray hairs with sorrow to the grave." Genesis 42:38

> "And now, behold, the king walketh before you: and I am old and grayheaded; and, behold, my sons are with you: and I have walked before you from my childhood unto this day." 1 Samuel 12:2

> "Now also when I am old and greyheaded, O God, forsake me not; until I have shewed thy strength unto this generation, and thy power to every one that is to come." Psalm 71:18

> *"Strangers have devoured his strength, and he knoweth it not: yea, gray hairs are here and there upon him, yet he knoweth not." Hosea 7:9*

## **<u>Brown</u>**

Brown is the color of wood, and when it is mentioned in the Word, it refers to decay and dead works.

> *"For other foundation can no man lay than that is laid, which is Jesus Christ. Now if any man build upon this foundation gold, silver, precious stones, wood, hay, stubble; Every man's work shall be made manifest: for the day shall declare it, because it shall be revealed by fire; and the fire shall try every man's work of what sort it is." 1 Corinthians 3:11-13*

> *"Therefore as the fire devoureth the stubble, and the flame consumeth the chaff, so their root shall be as rottenness, and their blossom shall go up as dust: because they have cast*

> *away the law of the LORD of hosts, and despised the word of the Holy One of Israel." Isaiah 5:24*

## Green

The color green represents growth and life. A green tree and green grass are signs of life.

> *"But I am like a green olive tree in the house of God: I trust in the mercy of God for ever and ever." Psalm 52:8*

> *"He maketh me to lie down in green pastures: he leadeth me beside the still waters. He restoreth my soul: he leadeth me in the paths of righteousness for his name's sake." Psalm 23:2-3*

The color green is obtained by mixing yellow and blue. Yellow represents joy, while blue represents Heaven. So, it is easy to gather that life comes to those who remain joyful through troubled times, whose focus is on obtaining the promise of Heaven. You don't always grow on the mountain top; sometimes you grow in the valley as you put your trust in the Lord.

## **White**

The color white is used to symbolize purity and overcoming trials of life.

> *"And I saw, and behold a white horse: and he that sat on him had a bow; and a crown was given unto him: and he went forth conquering, and to conquer." Revelation 6:2*

> *"Purge me with hyssop, and I shall be clean: wash me, and I shall be whiter than snow." Psalm 51:7*

> *"He that hath an ear, let him hear what the Spirit saith unto the churches; To him that overcometh will I give to eat of the hidden manna, and will give him a white stone, and in the stone a new name written, which no*

*man knoweth saving he that receiveth it." Revelation 2:17*

White is used in the Bible to describe:
- Teeth, Genesis 49:12
- Manna, Exodus 16:31
- Animals, Genesis 30:35; Revelation 6:2
- Baskets, Genesis 40:16
- Linen, 2 Chronicles 5:12
- Snow, Psalm 51:7
- Milk, Lamentations 4:7
- Fields, John 4:35
- Clouds, Revelation 14:14
- Thrones, Revelation 20:11
- Hair, Matthew 5:36

## **Orange**

The color orange is one of my favorite colors. It represents the fire of God and the continual construction of mankind into the image of Christ.

*"For our God is a consuming fire." Hebrews 12:29*

It is also used in the Bible in connection with:
- Iron, Psalm 2:9
- Pottery, Daniel 2:42-43

## Silver

Silver is used almost 100 times in the Bible in reference to testing and refining.

> *"Behold, I have refined thee, but not with silver; I have chosen thee in the furnace of affliction." Isaiah 48:10*

> *"The words of the Lord are pure words: as silver tried in a furnace of earth, purified seven times." Psalm 12:6*

> *"For thou, O God, hast proved us: thou hast tried us, as silver is tried." Psalm 66:10*

> *"The fining pot is for silver, and the furnace for gold: but the Lord trieth the hearts." Proverbs 17:3*

Silver was also used in the Bible in connection with:

- Silver shrines for Diana, Acts 19:24
- Commodities of trade, Ezekiel 27:12
- Plates, Jeremiah 10:9
- Coins, Genesis 20:16
- Cup/Jewelry, Genesis 44:2
- Fittings for Tabernacle, Exodus 26

## Brass

For the most part, brass in the Bible is synonymous with copper, bronze, and tin. When it is mentioned in the Bible, it refers to strength.

> *"He was a widow's son of the tribe of Naphtali, and his father was a man of Tyre, a worker in brass: and he was filled with wisdom, and understanding, and cunning to work all works in brass. And he came to king Solomon,*

*and wrought all his work." 1 Kings 7:14*


*"And I will break the pride of your power; and I will make your heaven as iron, and your earth as brass:" Leviticus 26:19*


*"And his feet like unto fine brass, as if they burned in a furnace; and his voice as the sound of many waters" Revelation 1:15*


Brass is also used in the Bible in connection to:

- Instruments, 1 Corinthians 13:1
- Purchasing other items, Ezekiel 27:13
- Utensils, 1 Kings 7:47
- Chains, Judges 16:21
- Statues, Daniel 2:32

## The Rainbow

A rainbow is a large arch of colors created by the light from the sun being broken up by water droplets in the atmosphere. The sun's light is white but the water droplets break it up into seven different colors:

>Red = Blood of Jesus
>Orange = Fire of God
>Yellow = Joy to the Lord
>Green = Growth
>Blue = Heaven
>Indigo = Wisdom
>Violet = Strength

Next time you see a rainbow, remember the promise of God but also remember what each color represents to our individual lives. The rainbow is a beautiful phenomenon, but it is also a sign of a promise that God will not destroy the world by flood again,

> *"And I, behold, I establish my covenant with you, and with your seed after you;*
>
> *And with every living creature that is with you, of the fowl, of the cattle, and of every beast of the earth with you; from all that go out of the ark, to every beast of the earth.*

"And I will establish my covenant with you, neither shall all flesh be cut off any more by the waters of a flood; neither shall there anymore be a flood to destroy the earth.

*And God said, This is the token of the covenant which I make between me and you and every living creature that is with you, for perpetual generations:*

*I do set my bow in the cloud, and it shall be for a token of a covenant between me and the earth.*

*And it shall come to pass, when I bring a cloud over the earth, that the bow shall be seen in the cloud:*

*And I will remember my covenant, which is between me and you and every living creature of all flesh; and the waters shall no more become a flood to destroy all flesh.*

*And the bow shall be in the cloud; and I will look upon it, that I may remember the everlasting covenant between God and every living creature of all flesh that is upon the earth.*

*And God said unto Noah, This is the token of the covenant, which I have established between me and all flesh that is upon the earth." Genesis 9:9-17*

Rainbows are also a sign of the second coming of Christ.

*"And I saw another mighty angel come down from heaven, clothed with a cloud: and a rainbow was upon his head, and his face was as it were the sun, and his feet as pillars of fire: And he had in his hand a little book open: and he set his right foot upon the sea, and his left foot on the earth," Revelation 10:1-2*

## Overview of Colors

| | | |
|---|---|---|
| Blue | = | Heaven |
| Black | = | Death and Mourning |
| Yellow | = | Joy and Warmth |
| Gold | = | Supremacy, Prosperity, and Authority |
| Red | = | Blood, Redemption, Sacrifice, and Love |
| Purple | = | Royalty and Wealth |
| Gray | = | Weakness and Wisdom |
| Brown | = | Decay and Dead Works |
| Green | = | Growth and Life |
| White | = | Purity and Overcoming Trials of Life |
| Orange | = | Fire of God and Continual Construction |
| Silver | = | Testing and Refining |
| Brass | = | Strength |
| Rainbow | = | Promise of God and the Second Coming of Christ |

# Chapter 3
## Significant Symbols of the Bible

Symbols are objects, signs, or animals that represent something of greater significance. Throughout the Bible, symbols are used by God to open up our understanding of the truths of God. God encourages us to be aware and knowledgeable of the meaning of the symbols used in the Word of God.

> *"Now all these things happened unto them for examples: and they are written for our admonition, upon whom the ends of the world are come." 1 Corinthians 10:11*

> *"For I have given you an example, that ye should do as I have done to you." John 13:15*

> *"The aged women likewise, that they be in behaviour as becometh holiness,*

*not false accusers, not given to much wine, teachers of good things; That they may teach the young women to be sober, to love their husbands, to love their children, To be discreet, chaste, keepers at home, good, obedient to their own husbands, that the word of God be not blasphemed." Titus 2:3-5*

*"And we desire that every one of you do shew the same diligence to the full assurance of hope unto the end: That ye be not slothful, but followers of them who through faith and patience inherit the promises." Hebrews 6:11-12*

*"For yourselves know how ye ought to follow us: for we behaved not ourselves disorderly among you; Neither did we eat any man's bread for nought; but wrought with labour and travail night and day, that we might not be chargeable to any of you: Not because we have not power, but to make ourselves an ensample*

*unto you to follow us." 2 Thessalonians 3:7-9*

## Objects

**Anchor** = Stability, Hebrews 6:18-19

**Ark of Covenant** = Presence of God, Exodus 25:10-22

**Armor** = Protection, Ephesians 6:10-17; Romans 13:12

**Arms** = Strength, Exodus 6:6

**Arrows** = Judgment, Psalm 38:2, 120:4

**Blood** = Life, Leviticus 17:11

**Bread** = Word of God, John 6:35, 51-52

**Cedar** = Power and Strength, Psalm 92:12

**Clay** = Flexibility, Isaiah 64:8

**Cross** = Suffering and Salvation, 1 Corinthians 1:8

**Crown** = Victory, 2 Kings 11:12; 2 Timothy 4:7-8

**Doors** = Opportunity, Revelation 3:20; Luke 12:24-25

**Dry Bones** = Death, Ezekiel 37:1-11

**Eyes** = Discernment, Matthew 13:10-17; 1 John 2:11

**Falling Stars** = Disobedience and Abandonment, Luke 10:18

**Feet** = Peace, Isaiah 52:7

**Fire** = Holy Spirit, Acts 2:3

**Fruit** = Production, Galatians 5:22

**Grass** = Rest or Weakness, Psalm 23, 90:5-6

**Hair** = Glory of God, 1 Corinthians 11:15

**Hands** = Power of God, 1 Peter 5:6

**Harlot** = False Church, Revelation 17:5-7

**Honey** = Happiness, Deuteronomy 8:8-9; Ezekiel 20:6

**Incense** = Prayers of Saints, Revelation 5:8

**Keys** = Binding and Loosing, Matthew 16:19

**Lamp** = Word of God, Psalm 119:105

**Milk** = Prosperity and Abundance, Ezekiel 25:4

**Mirror** = Revelation and Reflection, James 1:23-27

**Mountains** = Governments and Kingdoms, Isaiah 2:2-4

**Oak** = Strength and Durability, Zechariah 11:2

**Oil** = Holy Spirit, Zechariah 4:2-6; Revelation 4:5

**Rainbow** = God's Covenant, Genesis 9:13

**Ring** = Authority, Esther 8:10

**Rock** = Stability, Psalm 18:2, 40:2

**Rod** = Correction, Psalm 2:9; Job 9:34

**Sackcloth** = Mourning, Genesis 37:34

**Salt** = Preservation and Flavor, Matthew 5:13

**Sand** = Multitudes, 1 Kings 4:20

**Seal** = Ownership, Ephesians 4:30

**Shield** = Defense, Psalm 84:9

**Stairway** = Going Upward with God, Genesis 28:11-13

**Stars** = Angels, Revelation 1:20

**Throne** = God's Glory, Revelation 4:2, 22:3

**Trumpets** = God's Voice, Psalm 29:3, 68:33

**Vineyard** = Bearing Fruit, Luke 20:9-16

**Water** = Everlasting Life, John 7:38-39; Revelation 22:17

**Wind** = Holy Spirit, John 3:8; Acts 2:2

**Wine** = Blood of Christ, Luke 5:37; Isaiah 5:1-7

**Women** = Church, Ephesians 5:23-27; 2 Corinthians 11:2

**Wool** = Comfort, Ezekiel 34:3

**Yoke** = Slavery, Galatians 5:1

## Animals

**Ants** = Diligence, Proverbs 6:6-8

**Bats** = Darkness and Evil, Leviticus 11:19

**Bears** = Destruction, 2 Kings 2:23-24; Daniel 7:5

**Behemoth** = Largeness, Job 40:15

**Bull** = Stubbornness, Jeremiah 31:18

**Calf** = Joy, 1 Samuel 28:24-25

**Camel** = Burdens, Leviticus 11:4

**Donkeys** = Stubbornness, Numbers 22:28-31

**Dove** = Holy Spirit, Mark 1:10; Hope, Genesis 8:8-12

**Eagle** = Determination and Patience, Isaiah 40:31

**Elephants** = Maturity, 1 Kings 10:18; 2 Chronicles 9:17

**Fish** = Souls, Mark 1:16-20

**Flies** = Nuisance, Ecclesiastes 10:1

**Fox** = Strife and Trouble, Song of Solomon 2:15; Ezekiel 13:4

**Frogs** = Plagues, Psalm 78:45

**Goat** = Unfaithfulness, Luke 15:29; Numbers 7:16

**Greyhound** = Speed and Hunting, Proverbs 30:31

**Horse** = War and Strength, Zechariah 9:10; Jeremiah 51:21

**Leopard** = Speed, Daniel 7:6

**Leopards** = Cunning and Sneaky, Jeremiah 5:6

**Lion** = Kingship, Judges 14:8

**Locust** = Destruction, Deuteronomy 28:38; Joel 1:4

**Owl** = Wisdom and Rest, Isaiah 34:11

**Ox** = Sacrifice, Proverbs 14:4

**Raven** = Scavengers and Seed Eaters, Genesis 8:7; Luke 12:24

**Roosters** = Watching and Warning, Mark 14:30

**Serpent** = Satan, Genesis 3:1; Psalm 58:4

**Sheep** = Followers, John 10:11

**Swine** = Dirty and Demonic, Matthew 8:31

**Whales** = Beauty and Reflection, Matthew 12:40

**Wolf** = Danger, Matthew 7:15

**Wolves** = Deception and Destruction, Matthew 7:15

## Signs

**666** = Antichrist, Revelation 13:18

**Circumcision** = Removing Waste, Romans 4:11; Genesis 17:10-11

**Dark Clouds** = Trouble, Matthew 24:30

**Dry Bones** = Death, Ezekiel 37:1-2

**Earthquakes** = Spiritual Shaking, Matthew 24:7; Revelation 6:12

**Famine** = Spiritual Decay and Malnourishment, Amos 8:11

**Hail** = Judgment, Isaiah 28:16-17

**Lifted Hands** = Submission, Psalm 63:4

**Lightning** = Revelation, Psalm 97:4

**Miracles** = Power of God, Matthew 12:38

**Morning Star** = Jesus, Revelation 22:16

**Rain** = Blessings, Leviticus 26:3-4

**Rainbow** = God's Faithfulness, Genesis 9:13

**Spitting** = Contempt and Cursing, Isaiah 50:6; Matthew 26:67

**Still Small Voice** = Truth, Isaiah 30:15; Exodus 33:14

**Tongues of Fire** = Baptism of Holy Spirit, Acts 2:3

# Chapter 4
## Significant Names of the Bible

Naming things is a way to introduce and identify yourself with others. Names matter because it tells people who we are and what we do. In this chapter we will focus in on some names and meanings of God and other people in the Bible.

### Names of God

**Abba** = Our Father, Mark 14:36

**Adonai** = God is in Charge, Genesis 15:2

**El Olam** = God is Everlasting, Genesis 21:3

**El Roi** = The God who Sees, Genesis 16:13

**El Shaddai** = God Almighty, Genesis 17:1

**Elohim** = God is the Creator, Genesis 1:1

**Jehovah Jireh** = The Lord Provides, Genesis 22:13-14

**Jehovah Nissi** = The Lord is My Banner, Exodus 17:15

**Jehovah Rapha** = The Lord is My Healer, Exodus 15:26

**Jehovah Shalom** = The Lord is My Peace, Judges 6:24

**Jehovah Shammah** = The Lord is Present, Exodus 48:35

**Jehovah Tsidkenu** = The Lord is Our Righteousness, Jeremiah 23:6

**Jehovah Uzi** = The Lord is My Strength, Psalm 28:7

**Yahweh** = God is Always There, Genesis 2:4

## Names of Jesus

**Alpha and Omega,** Revelation 22:13
**Author and Finisher of Faith,** Hebrews 12:2
**Branch,** Isaiah 4:2
**Deliverer,** 1 Thessalonians 1:10
**Faithful and True,** Revelation 19:11
**Head of the Church,** Ephesians 1:22
**Immanuel,** Matthew 1:23

**Indescribable Gift,** 2 Corinthians 9:15
**King of Kings and Lord of Lords,** Revelation 17:14
**King of the Jews,** Matthew 2:1-2
**Lion of the Tribe of Judah,** Revelation 5:5
**Lord,** Acts 2:25
**Mediator,** 1 Timothy 2:5
**Messiah,** John 1:41
**Morning Star,** Revelation 22:16
**Our Hope,** 1 Timothy 1:1
**Prince of Peace,** Isaiah 9:6-7
**Rabbi,** John 1:38
**Resurrection and Life,** John 11:25
**Savior,** Luke 2:11
**Seed of Abraham,** Galatians 3:16
**Son of God,** John 10:34-42
**Son of Man,** Luke 19:10
**The Almighty One,** Revelation 1:8
**The Bread of Life,** John 6:35
**The Bridegroom,** John 3:29
**The Capstone,** Matthew 21:42
**The Chief Cornerstone,** 1 Peter 2:1-10

**The Deliverer,** 1 Thessalonians 1:10
**The Door,** John 10:9
**The Firstborn from the Dead,** Revelation 1:5
**The Good Shepherd,** John 10:11-18
**The Heir of all Things,** Hebrews 1:2
**The Horn of Salvation,** Luke 1:69
**The Lamb of God,** Revelation 5:6-14
**The Last Adam,** Revelation 3:14
**The Light of the World,** John 8:1-12
**The Lion of Judah,** Revelation 5:5
**The Rock,** 1 Corinthians 10:4
**The Root and Offspring of David,** Revelation 22:16
**The Vine,** John 15:1-9
**The Way,** John 14:6
**The Word,** John 1:1
**True Vine,** John 15:1
**Truth,** John 8:32

## Names, or Symbols, of the Holy Spirit

**Dove,** Matthew 3:16

**Fire,** Acts 2:3
**Oil,** Acts 10:38
**Water,** John 7:38
**Wind,** John 3:8
**Wine,** Ephesians 5:18

## Names of Satan

**Adversary** = Against righteousness, 1 Peter 5:8

**Angel of Light** = Refers to false prophets and teachers, 2 Corinthians 11:14

**Apollyon** = Destroyer, Revelation 9:11

**Beelzebub** = Lord of flies or lord of the manure, Matthew 12:24

**Belial** = Used in connection with filthiness and wickedness, 2 Corinthians 6:15

**Devil** = Tempter, Matthew 4:1-11

**Dragon** = Deadly, poisonous, ready to strike and kill creature, Revelation 12:9

**Evil one** = Found in the Lord's Prayer to describe to Satan, Matthew 6:13

**Father of Lies** = First lie found in Genesis 3:1; John 8:44

**Lucifer** = Light-bearer; shining one, Isaiah 14:12

**Murderer** = Jesus called him a murderer, John 8:44

**Prince of Power of the Air** = One who holds the highest seat of power, Ephesians 2:2

**Satan** = Adversary; enemy who hates, Job 1:6-22


## Names of Men

**Aaron** = Exalted one, Exodus 4-6
- A spokesman for Moses
- His rod produced miracles
- First High Priest


**Abel** = Breath, Genesis 4:1-16
- Second child of Adam and Eve
- First person murdered in the Bible

**Abner** = My Father is Light, 1 Sam 14:50, 17:55
- He was a cousin of Saul

- He killed Asahel; then Asahel's brother killed him

**Abraham** = Father of the Multitudes, Genesis 17
- Father of Israel
- His name was changed to Abraham from Abram to signify an increase of blessing and responsibility
- 99 years old when God's promise was fulfilled

**Absalom** = My Father is Peace, 2 Samuel 13
- Son of King David
- Murdered his sister's rapist
- Rebelled against his father
- Died when his hair got caught in a tree

**Achan** = Trouble, Joshua 7
- Praise and worship leader under Joshua
- Was stoned to death for stealing forbidden possession and hiding his sin

**Adam** = Man; Red clay, Genesis 2-3
- First man to be created
- First man to rebel against God by eating of the tree of knowledge

**Agrippa** = Wild Horse, Acts 26
- Grandson of Herod the great
- New Testament refers to him as Herod Agrippa
- Killed apostles of Christ

**Ahab** = Weak Man, 1 Kings 21
- Weak husband of Jezebel
- Elijah held him accountable for wicked behavior

**Amos** = Carried, Amos 1-9
- One of the 12 minor prophets
- A farmer by trade
- His message was one that spoke against greed and corruption.

**Ananias** = Vow breaker, Acts 5
- Husband of Sapphira

- Lied, stole, and tried to see how much he could get away with before being judged
- Was struck down dead in church because of disobedience

**Andrew** = Masculine Man, John 1:35-42, 6:4-14
- First disciple of Christ
- Fisherman by trade
- Brother of Simon Peter
- Brought the boy with five loaves and two fishes to Jesus

**Aquila** = Eagle, Acts 18:2-3
- Paul lived with him for a while in Acts
- Husband of Priscilla

**Asa** = Strength in God, 2 Chronicles 14
- Third king of Judah

**Asher** = Happy and blessed, Genesis 30:13
- Son of Jacob and Leah's handmaiden, Zilpah

**Barak** = Lightening, Judges 4-5
- Military commander under Deborah
- He united the tribes of Israel
- Listed as a hero of Faith in Hebrews 11

**Barnabas** = Son of Encouragement, Acts 4:36
- Missionary
- Accompanied Paul on missionary trips
- Encouraged John Mark when he was released from ministry by Paul

**Bartholomew** = Son of a Farmer, John 1:43-51
- One of the original 12 disciples of Christ
- Possibly a missionary to India after the death and resurrection of Christ
- Also known as Nathanael

**Benjamin** = Son of the Right-Handed, Gen. 35:18
- Twelfth and youngest son of Jacob
- His mother, Rachel, died shortly after giving birth to him

**Boaz** = Swift redeemer, Ruth 1-4
- Married Ruth
- Boaz was loving, loyal, and faithful

**Cain** = to Spear; Possessed, Genesis 8:1-15
- First son of Adam and Eve
- First murderer; killed his brother
- His consequences for murder was to be homeless and wander the earth without finding a place of rest

**Caleb** = Wholehearted, Numbers 13-14
- One of the 12 spies sent out to Canaan
- Very positive and strong person
- Faithful companion of Joshua
- Caleb and Joshua were the only two to live and enter into the Promised Land

**Cornelius** = Horn of God, Acts 10
- He was the first Gentile convert of Peter
- Great family man

**Daniel** = God is My Judge, Daniel 1-12

- A Hebrew prophet who has a book named after him in the Bible
- He lived during the Jewish captivity in Babylon where he served the king

**David** = Beloved of God, 1 Samuel 16:22

- Second greatest King of Israel
- Writer for at least half of the book of Psalms
- Defeated Goliath in perhaps the greatest Bible story ever
- A man after God's own heart

**Eli** = My God has Ascended, 1 Samuel 3

- The High Priest for Israel in the books of 1st and 2nd Samuel
- Gave guidance and direction to young Samuel
- Experienced a horrible, premature death due to bad parenting: he did not hold his children accountable

**Eliezer** = God is my Helper, Exodus 18:4

- Servant of Abraham
- Son of Moses

**Elijah** = Jehovah is My God, 1 Kings 17-22
- The greatest of all prophets
- Active during 9th century B.C. during the reign of King Ahab and Queen Jezebel
- A confronter of evil and a miracle worker
- Elijah appeared next to Jesus during transfiguration

**Elisha** = God is My Salvation, 2 Kings 2-6
- Understudy of Elijah and succeeded him after his ascension
- Prophet and miracle worker
- Performed twice as many recorded miracles (18) as Elijah in fulfillment of prophecy

**Ethan** = Firm and Stable, Psalm 89 NIV
- Author of Psalm 89
- Known as a Man of Wisdom

**Eutychus** = Good Fortune, Acts 20
- Fell asleep on Paul while he preached and fell from a third story window to

his death. Later, he was resurrected from the dead.
- A young man in ministry

**Ezekiel** = God Strengthens, Ezekiel 1-48
- Major Prophet in Old Testament with a book of the Bible attributed to his name
- Lived in Jerusalem until the Babylonians took Israel captive
- Straight forward, honest, and direct in his prophecies

**Felix** = Successful or Lucky, Acts 24
- Governor of Judea who imprisoned Paul
- Ruled by the "letter of the law"

**Gabriel** = Word-Bringer, Luke 1
- Interpreted the visions of the prophet Daniel
- Announced the birth of John to Zechariah
- Announced the birth of Jesus to Mary

**Gamaliel** = Benefit of God, Acts 5:34, 22:3
- Leader in church of New Testament
- Teacher of Apostle Paul

**Gideon** = Tough-skinned one, Judges 6:8
- Judge in Old Testament
- Led a small group of 300 Israelites in victory against 135,000 Midianites

**Habakkuk** = Embrace, Habakkuk 1-3
- One of the 12 minor prophets in the Old Testament
- Author of the book in the Bible, Habakkuk

**Haggai** = Festive One, Haggai 1-2
- One of the 12 minor prophets in the Old Testament with a book named after him
- Encouraged Israel to rebuild the temple after returning from Babylonian exile

**Hosea** = Salvation and Deliverance, Hosea 1-14

- Prophesied to the Northern Kingdom
- One of the 12 minor prophets in the Old Testament
- His story of dealing with an unfaithful wife parallels God's story with the unfaithful church

**Jonathan** = Faithful and Gift of God, 1 Samuel 13, 18
- Eldest son of King Saul
- Armor bearer to David
- Killed in battle with Philistines

**Isaac** = To Laugh and Rejoice, Genesis 17:19
- The promised child
- Almost offered as a sacrifice to God by Abraham

**Isaiah** = God is Salvation, Isaiah 1-66
- One of four major prophets of the Old Testament with an entire book of the Bible named after him
- Prophesied when Assyria threatened the Kingdom of Judah

**Jabez** = Sorrow, 1 Chronicles 4:9-10

- Uses prayer to change the momentum of his life
- Refused to allow past circumstances or current situations to negatively affect his life

**Jacob** = Deceiver, Genesis 27:19-32
- Son of Isaac and Rebekah
- Father of the twelve tribes of Israel
- Born holding his twin brother's heel

**James** = One who grasps and presses forward, Matthew 4:21; James 1-5
- Several people are called James in the Bible
- One was the brother of Jesus
- Another was beheaded in the book of Acts by Herod Agrippa

**Jason** = Healer and Helper, Acts 17:5-10
- A servant of the Lord to leaders within the church
- Gave shelter to Paul and Silas

**Jeremiah** = God has lifted high, Jeremiah 1-52

- Known as the "weeping prophet"
- Author of two books of the Bible, Jeremiah and Lamentations

**Jethro** = Abundance, Exodus 18

- A Midianite priest who helped Moses when he fled Egypt
- Moses' father in law

**Job** = Persecuted One, Job 1-42

- Only man called "perfect" in the Bible
- Known most for suffering great hardships and tragedy
- God doubled what he lost near the end of his life

**Joel** = Jehovah is God, Joel 1-3

- One of 12 Old Testament prophets
- Believed in an end-time revival for God's people

**John** = Beloved or God is Gracious, John 1-21

- Two main characters named John in the Bible, John the Baptist and Apostle John
- John the Baptist was the forerunner of Christ who baptized Jesus
- The apostle John was part of Jesus' inner circle and the writer of the book of John and Revelation

**Jonah** = Dove, Jonah 1-4

- A prophet who was swallowed by a "great fish" to save his life
- Commanded to preach to Nineveh

**Joseph** = God Adds, Genesis 37 – 44

- $11^{th}$ son of Jacob but the first son he had with his wife Rachel
- Favorite son of Jacob
- Had a coat of many colors

**Joshua** = Yahweh is Salvation, Joshua 1-24

- Old Testament companion of Moses who later succeeded Moses as leader
- Led Israel into the Promised Land

**Lemuel** = Belongs to God, Proverbs 31

- A king mentioned in Proverbs 31 whose mother gave him traits to look for in a "virtuous woman"
- Strong and quiet leader
- A king that did not drink alcohol


**Levi** = Joined together, Genesis 34:24-30

- Third son of Jacob and Leah
- Ancestor of one of the 12 tribes, Levites
- Levites provided the priests for Israel


**Lot** = Covering, Genesis 18-19

- He was Abraham's nephew
- Directed to leave Sodom and Gomorrah without looking back
- His wife looked back and turned into a pillar of salt


**Luke** = Trained or sophisticated one, Acts 1:28; Luke 1-24

- A doctor by trade
- Author of books, Luke and Acts, in the New Testament

**Malachi** = God's Messenger, Malachi 1-4

- One of the 12 minor prophets in the Old Testament
- A prophet of God who proclaimed the coming of Christ

**Mark** = Consecrated to God, Mark 1-16

- Author of the second gospel in the New Testament
- Could possibly be the same person as John Mark in book of Acts

**Matthew** = Gift of God, Matthew 1-28

- One of 12 disciples
- A tax collector by trade

**Matthias** = Gift from God, Acts 1:12-26

- The 13th disciple that replaced Judas Iscariot
- Declared as the new disciple at Pentecost

**Methuselah** = Man of the Dart, Genesis 5:21-27
- Father of Lamech and grandfather of Noah
- Lived 969 years, making him the person to live the longest in the Bible

**Micah** = Who is like God, Micah 1-7
- One of the 12 minor prophets
- Author of the book of Micah which offers both prophecies of destruction and prophecies of restoration

**Michael** = Who is like God, Daniel 10:13; Jude 9
- An Archangel in the Bible
- Warfare Angel of the Bible

**Moses** = Deliverer, Exodus 1-40
- Pulled out of the Nile River by Pharaoh's daughter and adopted by the royal family
- He demanded the release of the Israelites from the Egyptians and Pharaoh

- Received the Ten Commandments from the Lord to give to His people
- He died before entering the Promise Land

**Nahum** = Comforter, Nahum 1-3

- One of 12 minor prophets in the Old Testament
- Authored the book of Nahum which prophesies the downfall of Nineveh

**Nicodemus** = Victory of the People, John 3

- Helped Joseph of Arimathea in the burial of Jesus
- A member of the Sanhedrin Council
- Came to speak with Jesus at night

**Noah** = Motion, Genesis 5-9

- Builder of the Ark that took 120 years to build
- Died 350 years after the flood
- Father of Shem, Ham, and Japheth

**Paul** = Small or Humble One, Acts 8-28

- Was born in Tarsus
- Was a persecutor of the church until he had a great encounter with the Lord
- Went on three missionary journeys and wrote 13 books of the New Testament

**Peter** = Stone, Matthew 16

- In the inner circle of relationship with Christ
- Mouthpiece for the disciples

**Philip** = Lover of horses, Acts 8:26-40

- An evangelist from the city of Bethsaida
- One of the 12 disciples in the New Testament

**Samson** = Sun child and brightness, Judges 13-16

- Great strength came from his long hair
- Seduced by Delilah who cut his hair off and betrayed him to the Philistines for money

**Saul** = Got what you asked for, 1 Samuel 9-22
- First King of Israel and Judah
- Tried to kill David because of his jealousy of him

**Solomon** = Peace, 1 Kings 3:4
- Known for his wealth and wisdom
- Authored Proverbs, Ecclesiastes, and the Song of Solomon
- King of Israel when he was a teenager
- Son of David and Bathsheba

**Stephen** = That which surrounds, Acts 7
- A deacon in the New Testament Church
- Became the first martyr in the Bible when he was stoned to death

**Thaddaeus** = All heart, Jude 1
- Also referred to as Jude
- One of the 12 disciples in the New Testament

**Thomas** = Twin, John 20:25
- Doubted Jesus' resurrection until he saw and examined His wounds himself.
- One of the 12 disciples in the New Testament

**Timothy** = Honors God, 1 and 2 Timothy
- Dedicated his life to the Lord at an early age
- Raised by his mother and grandmother
- A trusted confidant of Paul

**Titus** = Honorable, Acts 15:2; Titus 1-3
- Accompanied Paul and Barnabas to the church council at Jerusalem
- Sent by Paul to Ephesus to collect money on behalf of the poor saints in Jerusalem

**Uriah** = God is My light, 2 Samuel 11
- A Hittite warrior in David's army
- The first husband of Bathsheba

**Zechariah** = God remembers, Zechariah 1-14
- An Old Testament prophet who authored the book of Zechariah
- Zechariah in the New Testament was the father of John the Baptist

**Zephaniah** = God is Hidden, Zephaniah 1-3
- One of the 12 minor prophets in the Old Testament who authored the book of Zephaniah
- The only prophet of royal descent

**Zimri** = My Praise, 1 Kings 12:1-24; 1 Kings 16:16
- King of Israel in the Old Testament who ruled for seven days
- Was succeeded by the commander of the army, Omri
- A chariot commander who murdered King Elah

# Names of Women

**Abigail** = My Father is Joy, 1 Samuel 25

- Third wife of David after Nabal, her first husband, died
- A servant who was a good cook
- A woman of beauty and brains

**Achsah** = Adorned with Beauty, Joshua 1; 1 Chronicles 4:15

- Daughter of Caleb
- She claimed additional blessing for her family because she was bold enough to ask for more

**Anna** = Gracious One, Luke 2:36-38

- Recognized Jesus as Messiah
- A prophetess in the New Testament who was an elderly Jew

**Deborah** = Bee, Judges 4:6-7
- Sweet as honey, but could sting like a bee
- Formed an army under the command of Barak

**Elizabeth** = My God is Abundance, Luke 1:5-7
- Mother of John the Baptist
- Helped Mary recover from depression

**Esther** = Star, Esther 1-10
- Jewish wife of the King of Persia
- Great ability to persuade others

**Eunice** = Good Victory, 2 Timothy 1:5
- Mother of Timothy in the New Testament
- More than likely raised Timothy as a single mom

**Eve** = To Live and Breathe, Genesis 1-3
- Created from Adam's rib
- Gave into temptation from the serpent in the Garden of Eden

**Hagar** = Flight, Genesis 16
- Sarah's Egyptian servant
- Mother of Ishmael

**Hannah** = Favored, 1 Samuel 1-2
- Woman of prayer and faith
- Believed for her barrenness to turn and God gave her a son

**Jehoshabeath** = Fullness of God, 2 Chronicles 22:11
- Daughter of King Jehoram
- Fled danger in order to protect her son from death

**Jezebel** = She-devil, 1 Kings 18-19
- Worshipped Baal and married to Ahab
- Main enemy of the great prophet Elijah
- A usurper of authority and a manipulative person

**Lydia** = Noble One, Acts 16:14, 40
- A convert of Paul to Christianity

- A seller of purple
- A woman of faith and hospitality

**Mary Magdalene** = Tower for God, Luke 7:36-50; Luke 23-24

- Delivered of many evil spirits
- Witnessed the crucifixion and resurrection

**Mary** = Wished for a Child and Beloved, Luke 1

- Mother of Jesus
- Present at Pentecost, Acts 1:14
- A woman of faith and a model disciple

**Martha** = The Lady, Luke 10:38-42

- Sister of Lazarus and Mary of Bethany

**Miriam** = Bitterness, Exodus 15; Numbers 12

- Moses' sister who was smart and confident
- Helped save her brother's life and set Israel's deliverance in motion

- She got leprosy when she and Aaron spoke against Moses, their brother

**Phoebe** = Pure or bright, Romans 16:1-2
- A female minister in the church of the New Testament
- A humble servant of the Lord

**Priscilla** = Ancient wise one, Acts 18:2-3
- Married to Aquilla and lived in Corinth
- Paul lived with her and her husband for a while in the book of Acts

**Rachel** = Little sheep, Genesis 29
- Favorite wife of Jacob
- Younger sister of Leah
- Mother of Joseph and Benjamin

**Rebekah** = To join together, Genesis 24
- Wife of Isaac and mother of Jacob and Esau

**Ruth** = Friend, Ruth 1-4
- A Moabite woman who was faithful to her mother in law after the death of her husband
- She met and married Boaz

# Chapter 5
## Significant Places of the Bible

God Created places before He created people. So, where you are is just as important as what God has called you to do. You cannot be in the wrong place and expect to receive the right blessing from the Lord. Places have an identity and character. Places can provide safety, sanctuary, and salvation. Places give us memories from our past, lessons for our present, and hope for our future.

Gaining a greater understanding of the places in the Bible is not just about geographical knowledge. Knowing what certain places mean and represent gives us insight that uncovers hidden truths that God desires to reveal. The places of the Bible have a message that unlocks mysteries to knowing God and drawing closer to Him.

**Adullam** = City of Safety
- A royal city that housed a king, Joshua 12:15
- Rehoboam fortified the city, 2 Chronicles 11:7
- Called "The glory of Israel", Micah 1:15
- David ran to Adullam and hid in a large cave to get safety from King Saul who was trying to kill him, 1 Samuel 22

**Ai** = Ruins
- Joshua and Israel were defeated in Ai because of the sin of Achan, Joshua 7
- Rebuilt and inhabited by the Benjamites, Ezra 2:28

**Antioch** = Landmark
- Disciples were first called Christians, Acts 11:26
- Connected to the early history of the church, Acts 6:5
- Paul and Barnabas visited Antioch on their first missionary journey, Acts 13:14

**Ararat** = Sacred High Land
- The mountain that Noah's Ark rested on after the flood waters began to subside, Genesis 8:4
- Ararat is translated as "Armenia" in the King James Bible, 2 Kings 19:37

**Arimathaea** = Dirt
- A Jewish city, Luke 23:51
- Birthplace of Joseph in whose tomb Jesus was buried, Matthew 27:57, 60

**Armageddon** = Valley of Megiddo
- Occurs only once in the Bible, Revelation 16:16
- The place of the final battle between Jesus and the Antichrist, Revelation 16:4-16

**Ashdod** = Stronghold
- Main areas of the worship of Dagon in Philistine, 1 Samuel 5:5
- Ashdod belonged to the tribe of Judah but they never took possession of it, Joshua 15:47

**Baalhamon** = Place of the multitude
- Solomon had a large vineyard in Baalhamon, Song of Solomon 8:11
- A beautiful and wealthy city, Song of Solomon 8:11

**Babel** = Confusion
- A city in Babylon, Genesis 11
- A large tower was built by the people who worked together in unity until God sent confusion to the city, Genesis 11

**Babylon** = The Gate of God
- Destruction to the city was prophesied, Isaiah 13; Daniel 2
- Cyrus issued a decree permitting the Jews to return to their own land, Ezra 1

**Baca** = Garbage dump
- A valley of weeping, Psalm 84:6
- A dirty place people passed through on their way to church, Psalm 84

**Bethany** = House of dates and palms

- A village on the slope of Mount Olives, Mark 11:1
- The place where Lazarus and his sisters lived, John 11

**Bethel** = House of God

- Was originally the royal Canaanite city of Luz, Genesis 28:19
- Jacob had a vision in Bethel of angels ascending and descending on a ladder, Genesis 28:10, 19
- Place where people went to seek counsel of God, Judges 20:18

**Bethlehem** = House of bread

- Place where Rachel died and was buried, Genesis 48:7
- David's birthplace and the place he was anointed as king, 1 Samuel 16:4-13
- Birthplace of Christ, Matthew 2:6

**Calvary** = Place of the skull
- The crucifixion of Christ took place outside the city walls, Hebrews 13:11-13
- Also called Golgotha

**Canaan** = Land of Promise
- A land that gets its name from the fourth son of Hem, Genesis 10:6
- Boundaries of Canaan mentioned in scripture, Genesis 10:19, 17:8; Numbers 13:29, 34:8

**Capernaum** = Nahum's town
- A large Galilean fishing village where Peter, Andrew, James, and John lived
- Jesus healed a demon-possessed man, Mark 1:21-28
- Jairus' daughter was raised from the dead, Mark 5:21-23

**Carmel** = The Park
- Place where Elijah called fire down from Heaven and killed the prophets of Baal, 1 Kings 18

- Elisha brought a boy back to life, 2 Kings 4:25-37
- A town in the hill country of Judah, Joshua 15:55

**Corinth** = Satisfied and Beautiful

- A city in Greece on the mainland, Acts 18
- This is where Paul met Aquilla and Priscilla
- Paul made two visits to Corinth, one in Acts 18 that lasted a year and a half and another in Acts 20 for three months

**Eden** = Delight

- The place where Adam and Eve were brought to life, lived, and worked, Genesis 2:8-17
- God forced Adam and Eve to leave the garden after sinning, Genesis 3:23-24

**Endor** = Fountain
- A Canaanite city that Israel failed to conquer. It was a territory of the tribe of Issachar, Joshua 17:11
- King Saul consulted a witch for advice in Endor, 1 Samuel 28:7

**Ephesus** = Desire
- One of seven churches of Revelation that Jesus sent a letter to, Revelation 3
- Distinguished for the goddess of Diana and her temple, 1 Corinthians 4, 8

**Gethsemane** = Oil Press
- The place of agony for Christ before the crucifixion, Mark 14:32
- A beautiful garden filled with olives that Jesus loved to go to spend time with His father, Luke 33:29

**Gilgal** = Rolling
- Abraham built his first altar in Gilgal, Genesis 12:6-7

- Place where Israelites encamped and had their first Passover after entering Canaan, Joshua 4-5

**Hades** = Place of the dead

- Is mentioned in Matthew 16:18 NIV, *"gates of Hades* (Hell) *shall not prevail."*
- Keys of Hades (Hell), Revelation 1:18 NIV

**Heaven** = Place of reward for righteousness

- Jesus called Heaven His Father's house, John 14:2
- Called Paradise, Luke 23:43

**Hebron** = A Community that fellowships

- Favorite home of Abraham where he buried his wife, Sarah, Genesis 23:17-20
- Place of David's royal residence for over seven years, 2 Samuel 5:5

**Hell** = The invisible place
- The home of the wicked, Numbers 16:33; Psalm 9:17
- Peter describes it as a prison, 1 Peter 3:18-19

**Jericho** = Walled City
- Strongest fortified and most important city in the Jordan Valley, Numbers 22:1
- City was given to the tribe of Benjamin, Joshua 18:21
- The walls of Jericho fell after Joshua marched around them seven times, Joshua 6

**Jerusalem** = City of God and Place of Peace
- Once called the city of Judah, 2 Chronicles 25:28
- City was set on fire by men of Judah, Judges 1:1-8
- David brought the head of Goliath to Jerusalem, 1 Samuel 17:54

**Jordan** = The Watering Place
- Place where Abraham and Lot separated, Genesis 13:10
- Place where Jesus was baptized, Mark 1:9
- Waters were divided by Elijah and Elisha, 2 Kings 2:8-14

**Mars Hill** = Rocky Place
- Paul preached a message on Mars Hill, Acts 17:22-31
- A very rocky and steep mountain

**Nazareth** = A Watch Tower
- Home of Mary and Joseph, Luke 2:39
- Angel announced to Mary the coming birth of Jesus, Luke 1:26-28

**Patmos** = Barrenness
- A small and barren island
- John was exiled on the island of Patmos, Revelation 1:9

**Philippi** = The Fountain
- Lydia, the business woman, lived in Philippi, Acts 16
- First European Church was in Philippi

**Sea of Galilee** = Unpredictable
- Called Sea of Chinnereth in the Old Testament, Numbers 34:11
- Luke called it "the Lake of Gennesaret," Luke 5:1
- John called it the "Sea of Tiberias," John 6:1
- Jesus calmed the storm on the Sea of Galilee, Matthew 8

**Zion** = Sunny
- David took Zion from the Jebusites, Joshua 15:63; 2 Samuel 5:7
- Known as, "the city of David," 1 Kings 8:1
- Zion represents the Church, Hebrews 12:22

# CONCLUSION

It's obvious that there is more to God and His Word than what initially meets the eye. There is a lot to be gained from a shallow first look at the Word of God, but for those wanting to dig deep, there are many rewards that will be revealed. If you are willing to take the time and make the effort, there are wonderful sides of God yet to be discovered by His people. Digging deeper in the Bible to find Truth will not only keep your relationship with God fresh, but it will provide the opportunity to understand the heart of God for particular situations. We have a right to have as much of the revelation of God as we desire. But remember, the more you know, the more you will be held accountable to apply the truths that God reveals.

> *"The secret things belong to the LORD our God, but the things revealed belong to us and to our children forever, that we may observe all the words of this law." Deuteronomy 29:29NIV*

We should gain knowledge from God's Word and pursue the Lord to leave a lasting legacy for our children. All good parents want more for their children then they had for themselves. Through our pursuit of knowing God more, we can pass a great inheritance down from generation to generation.

This book was birthed from a heart with a desire to understand the Lord more and create in others a passion to draw closer to the Lord through exciting scripture-based revelations. My hope is that you will look at the Word of God a little differently after reading this book. Always be conscience when studying the Word of God of personal messages God would like to speak to you. GOD STILL SPEAKS!!! And He wants to speak to you! Unlocking the mysteries of God is the heart of God. A reward to those who diligently seek him with their whole heart. Being familiar with and having an understanding of numbers, colors, symbols, names, and places of the Bible will only increase your ability to know God more. If those things are in the Bible, then they are there for a reason, and not put in there by accident. So, use this book as a resource tool to refer back to when reading the Word of God to fully understand a particular passage or story in the Bible. What I have provided for you in this book only scratches the surface. What lies ahead is greater understanding from the things in God's Word. I pass the baton on to you to carry on the work of this book to research, study, and go beyond the surface to continue to unlock the mysteries of God.

www.ingramcontent.com/pod-product-compliance
Lightning Source LLC
Chambersburg PA
CBHW051452290426
44109CB00016B/1721